DIANETICS
THE EVOLUTION OF A SCIENCE

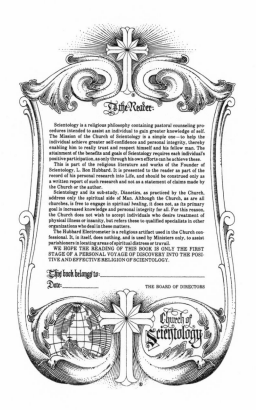

Important Note

In studying Dianetics and Scientology be very, very certain you never go past a word you do not fully understand.

The only reason a person gives up a study or becomes confused or unable to learn is that he or she has gone past a word or phrase that was not understood.

Trying to read past a misunderstood word results in mental "fogginess" and difficulty in comprehending the passages which follow. If you find yourself experiencing this, return to the last portion you understood easily, locate the misunderstood word and get it defined correctly—and then go on.

DIANETICS®: From the Greek dia (through) and noos *(soul), thus "through the soul"; a system for the analysis, control and development of human thought which also provides techniques for increased ability, rationality, and freedom from the discovered single source of aberrations and psychosomatic ills. Introduced May, 1950, with publication of* Dianetics: The Modern Science of Mental Health *by L. Ron Hubbard.*

SCIENTOLOGY® is an applied religious philosophy and technology resolving problems of the spirit, life and thought; discovered, developed and organized by L. Ron Hubbard as a result of his earlier Dianetic discoveries. Coming from the Latin, scio *(knowing) and the Greek* logos *(study), Scientology means "knowing how to know" or "the study of wisdom."*

DIANETICS®

THE EVOLUTION OF A SCIENCE

by

L. Ron Hubbard

PUBLICATIONS ORGANIZATION
UNITED STATES

Published by
The Church of Scientology of California
Publications Organization U.S.
4833 Fountain Avenue, East Annex
Los Angeles, California 90029

The Church of Scientology is a non-profit organization.
Scientology is an applied religious philosophy.
Dianetics® and Scientology® are registered names.

Reprinted October, 1979

ISBN 0-88404-017-8

dianetics

A Dianetics Publication. Dianetics is the trademark of L. Ron
Hubbard in respect of his published works.

Printed in the United States of America

Dianetics: The Evolution of a Science was the first broad publication of a subject of great importance to mankind.

Issued as a book-length feature in a national magazine it received a startlingly immediate and wide response from scientists, engineers and the general public. Telling the story of a major branch of L. Ron Hubbard's research it came as something of a "preview of the avalanche".

The avalanche was *Dianetics: The Modern Science of Mental Health*.

Published in May, 1950, *Dianetics* shot to the top of the best-seller lists across the country and stayed there week after week and month after month—and has been a continuing best-seller of international importance ever since.

World response to Dianetics was typically expressed in terms like those of the *New York Times* review of *Dianetics: The Modern Science of Mental Health*: "As with all great books, the impact of Dianetics means the world will never be the same again. History has become a race between Dianetics and catastrophe. Dianetics will win if enough people are challenged, in time, to understand it."

While the psychiatric associations publicly set up a dissident howl, an enormous number of individual psychiatrists privately described Hubbard's work as the first validly workable technology in the field of the mind.

Within less than two years following *Evolution of a Science*, having made a swift series of technical advances in Dianetics, Hubbard was suddenly and decisively breaking through into the vast new echelon of thought and existence which came to be known as Scientology (from the Latin *scio*—knowing, in the fullest sense of the word, plus the Greek *logos*—study; thus by the nature of its area of research, its methodology and its application, a religious philosophy and technology).

A long-time best-seller in its own right, *Dianetics: The Evolution of a Science* is a uniquely valuable work giving an understanding of how Hubbard was able to bring precision and workability to the customarily inexact subject of philosophy and the human mind.

"In the early fifties", Hubbard has said recently, "new discoveries concerning Life origin and destination brought us to Scientology. But Dianetics was never lost sight of, and every little while I would push it further ahead toward a fast, easy 100% workability." Thus we have had, since 1969, a Standard Dianetics, which routinely produces the result of a well and happy, high-I.Q. human being. It is being done successfully by many, many thousands across the planet today.

Given the phenomenon known as "cultural lag", Dianetics and Scientology may well be, as some commentators have said, a hundred years ahead of their time, but one might better say that they have arrived just in time—before we all go up in smoke.

Without question comparable in its importance to Scientology, Dianetics is a science in the fullest sense of the word. With its training courses filled with people from all walks of life, all types of backgrounds, Dianetics is a highly successful activity and expanding internationally.

This book is the story of how a man brought this new science into existence.

Dianetics
The Evolution of a Science

The optimum computing machine is a subject which many of us have studied. If you were building one, how would you design it?

First, the machine should be able to compute with perfect accuracy on any problem in the Universe and produce answers which were always and invariably right.

Second, the computer would have to be swift, working much more quickly than the problem and process could be vocally articulated.

Third, the computer would have to be able to handle large numbers of variables and large numbers of problems simultaneously.

Fourth, the computer would have to be able to evaluate its own data and there would have to remain available within it not only a record of its former conclusions but the evaluations leading to those conclusions.

Fifth, the computer would have to be served by a memory bank of nearly infinite capacity in which it could store observational data, tentative conclusions which might serve future computations and the data in the bank would have to be available to the analytical portion of the computer in the smallest fractions of a second.

Sixth, the computer would have to be able to rearrange former conclusions or alter them in the light of new experience.

Seventh, the computer would not need an exterior program director but would be entirely self-determined about its programming guided only by the necessity-value of the solution which it itself would determine.

Eighth, the computer should be self-servicing and self-arming against present and future damage and would be able to estimate future damage.

Ninth, the computer should be served by perception by which it could determine necessity-value. The equipment should include means of contacting all desirable characteristics in the finite world. This would mean color-visio, tone-audio, odor, tactile and self perceptions—for without the last it could not properly service itself.

Tenth, the memory bank should store perceptions as perceived, consecutive with time received with the smallest possible time divisions between perceptions. It would then store in color-visio (moving), tone-audio (flowing), odor, tactile and self sensation, all of them cross-co-ordinated.

Eleventh, for the purposes of solutions, it would have to be able to create new situations and imagine new perceptions hitherto not perceived and should be able to conceive these to itself in terms of tone-audio, color-visio, odor, tactile and self sensation and should be able to file anything so conceived as imagined labeled memories.

Twelfth, its memory banks should not exhaust on inspection but should furnish to the central perceptor of the computer, without distortion, perfect copies of everything and anything in the banks in color-visio, tone-audio, odor, tactile and organic sensations.

Thirteenth, the entire machine should be port-able.

There are other desirable characteristics but those listed above will do for the moment.

It might be somewhat astonishing, at first, to conceive of such a computer. But the fact is, the machine is in existence. There are about two billion of them in use today and many, many more billions have been made and used in the past.

In fact, you've got one. For we are dealing with the human mind.

The above is a generalization of the optimum brain. The optimum brain, aside from the fact that it is not always capable of solving every problem in the Universe, basically works exactly like that. It should have color-visio (in motion), tone-audio (flowing), odor, tactile and organic memory recall. And it should have color-visio (in motion), tone-audio (flowing), odor, tactile and organic imagination, also recallable after imagining like any other memory. And it should be able to differentiate between actuality and imagination with precision. And it should be able to recall any perception, even the trivial, asleep and awake from the beginning of life to death. That is the optimum brain, that and much, much more. It should think with such swiftness that vocal pondering would be utterly unable to keep pace with a thousandth part of one computation. And, modified by viewpoint and educational data, it should be *always* right, its answers *never* wrong.

That is the brain you have, potentially. That is the brain which can be restored to you unless you have had some section of it removed. If it does not do these things, it is slightly out of adjustment.

It took a long time to arrive at the data that this was an optimum brain. In the beginning it was not realized that some people had color-visio—moving—recall, for instance, and that some did not. I had no idea that many people imagined, and knew they were imagining, in tone-audio, et cetera, and would have received with surprise the data that somebody could smell and taste last Thanksgiving's turkey when he recalled it.

Fifteen years ago, when the researches which culminated in Dianetics (Gr. *dianoua* thought) were

Dianetics:

started in earnest, no such high opinion of the human brain was held. In fact, the project was not begun to trace function and restore optimum operation, but to know the key to human behavior and the code law which would reduce all knowledge.

My right to enter this field was an inquiring brain which had been trained in mathematics and engineering and which had a memory bank full of questions and far-flung observations.

It was the basic contention that the human mind was a problem in engineering and that all knowledge would surrender to an engineering approach.

And another primary assumption was made:

All answers are basically simple.

As it stands today, the science of Dianetics and its results—which are as demonstrable as the proposition that water, at fifteen pounds per square inch and 212° F., boils—is an engineering science, built heuristically* on axioms.** It works. That is the

---

Heuristic: serving to guide, discover or reveal.
**Axiom:* a proposition regarded as a self-evident truth.

only claim for Dianetics or chemistry. They may not be True. But they work and work invariably in the finite world.

When the problem had been shuffled around, in the beginning, and when questions had been formulated to be asked of the Universe at large, there was no concept of the optimum brain. Attention was fixed upon the *normal* brain. The *normal* brain was considered to be the optimum brain. Attempts were made, when work finally got around to the problem of the brain itself, to obtain results comparable with the normal mind. Minds became aberrated.* When restored they would be normal.

In fact, in the beginning, it was not even certain that minds could be restored. All that was required was an answer to existence and the reasons minds aberrated.

In a lifetime of wandering around many strange things had been observed. The medicine man of the Goldi People of Manchuria, the shamans of North Borneo, Sioux medicine men, the cults of Los Angeles, and modern psychology. Amongst the

---

*A*berrated: departed from rationality, deranged.

people questioned about existence were a magician whose ancestors served in the court of Kublai Khan and a Hindu who could hypnotize cats. Dabbles had been made in mysticism, data had been studied from mythology to spiritualism. Odds and ends like these, countless odds and ends.

If you were constructing this science, where would you have started? Here were all the various cults and creeds and practices of a whole world to draw upon. Here were facts to a number which makes 10^{21} binary digits look small. If you were called upon to construct such a science and to come up with a workable answer, what would you have assumed, gone to observe, or computed?

Everybody and everything seemed to have a scrap of the answer. The cults of all the ages, of all the world seem, each one, to contain a fragment of the truth. How do we gather and assemble the fragments? Or do we give up this nearly impossible task and begin postulating our own answers?

Well, this is the story of how Dianetics was built. This, at least, was the approach made to the problem. Dianetics works, which is what an engineer asks, and it works all the time, which is what nature demands of the engineer.

First, attempts were made to discover what school or system was workable. Freud did occasionally. So did Chinese acupuncture. So did magic healing crystals in Australia and miracle shrines in South America. Faith healing, voodoo, narco-synthesis— and, understand this right here, no mystic mumbo jumbo need apply. An engineer has to have things he can measure. Later the word "demon" is used. That's because Socrates describes one so well. Dianetic use of it, like Clerk-Maxwell's, is descriptive slang. But no wild immeasurable guesses or opinions were wanted. When an engineer uses only those, bridges break, buildings fall, dynamos stop and a civilization goes to wrack.

A primary need, in arriving at a dynamic principle of existence, was to discover what one wanted to know about existence. One does not have to dabble long with the gods to know that they point unvaryingly if divinely up a very blind alley. And an engineering study of mysticism demonstrates that mysticism embraces largely what it cannot hope to state precisely.

The first proposition went off something on this

Dianetics:

order. Let us find out what we cannot consider or do not need to consider to get an answer we can use. Some tests seemed to demonstrate that the exact identity of the Prime Mover Unmoved was not necessary to the computation. Man has been convinced for a long time that He started this affair, so no great gain could be made in getting disputive about it. Let us then take a level immediately below the Prime Mover Unmoved.

Now let us see what else falls into the category of data unnecessary to the computation. Well, we've studied telepathy, demons, the Indian rope trick and the human soul and so far we have yet to find any constants in this class of data. So let us draw a line below that as our highest level of necessary information and now call this our highest line.

What do we have left? We have the finite world, blue serge suits, Salinas Valley, the Cathedral at Rheims as a building and several decayed empires and roast beef for dinner. We have left only what we can perceive with no higher level of abstraction.

Now, how do we perceive and on what and with what? Ensues here a lot of time spent—1937—in computing out the brain as an electronic calculator

16

with the probable mathematics of its operation plus the impossibility of such a structure capable of doing such things. Let us then rule out the necessity of knowing structure and use this as an analogy only which can become a variable in the equation if necessary.

Now what do we have? Well, we've been a little hard on demons and the human soul. These are popular but they refuse to stand out and submit to a thorough inspection and caliper mensuration and if they won't so cooperate, then neither will we. And so two things come from this reduction of equation factors necessary to solution. First, existence is probably finite and second, finite factors alone answered the need of the problem.

Probably we could be very obtuse and mathematical here, but no matter. A good, workable heuristic principle, a *workable* one, is worth an infinity of formulas based on Authority and opinions which do *not* work.

All we can do is try the principle. We need a dynamic principle of existence. We look in Spencer and we find something which reads awfully good. It read good when he took it from Indian writings, the same place Lucretius got it. But it only pretends to be dynamic because it doesn't compute. We need a *dynamic* principle, not a description.

But what does a principle mean in a sphere this large? And doesn't it need a better definition? Let us then call it a dynamic lowest common denominator of existence.

Will such a lowest common denominator lead us straight up above the highest level we have set and send us spinning off with a fist full of variables and no answer? It had better not. So let us pose some more questions and see if they clarify the principle.

What can we know? Can we know where life came from? Not just now. Can we know where life is going? Well, that would be interesting but few of us will live to see that. So what can we know? Who, when, why, where, what—WHAT! We can know WHAT life is doing.

Let us postulate now that life started somewhere and is going somewhere. To know where it came from might solve a lot of problems but that seems unnecessary to know at this time for this problem. And the somewhere it's going might be known too some day but again we do not need to know that. So now we have something for the equation which will stay in terms of constants. WHAT is life doing enroute?

Life is energy of some sort. The purpose seems to involve energy. We are being heuristic. No arguments necessary because all we want is something with a high degree of workability, that's all any scientist needs. If this won't work, we'll dream up another one and postulate until something does work.

What is energy doing? It's surviving—changing form, but surviving.

What is life doing? It's surviving.

Now maybe it is doing a whole lot more, but we'll just try this on for size. What is the lowest common denominator of all existence which we have so far found?

SURVIVE!

The only test of an organism is survival.

That can be computed.

Dianetics:

We can even go so far as to make it colorful and say that there was a beginning of track and at this beginning of track Somebody said SURVIVE! He didn't say why and He didn't say until. All He said was SURVIVE!

Well, that's simple and it computes. It makes sense on the slide rule and it makes sense with a lot of activity and it seems pretty good—let's see.

The brain was a computer-director evolved on the same principles and on the same plan as cells and by cells and is composed of cells. The brain resolved problems relating to survival, asked itself questions about survival, acted upon its own best conceived but personally viewpointed plan for survival.

If one sagged down towards unsurvival, one was goaded up the scale toward survival by pain. One was lured ahead by pleasure into survival. There was a graduated scale with one end in death and the other in immortality.

The brain thought in terms of differences, similarities and identities and all its problems were resolved on these lines and all these problems and all these activities were strictly and solely survival-motivated. The basic command data on which the body and brain operated was SURVIVE! That was all; nothing fell outside this.

It was postulated to see if it worked.

That was in 1938 after several years of study. The axioms began with SURVIVE! SURVIVE was the lowest common denominator of all existence. They proceeded through axioms as to what Man was doing and how he was doing it. Nice definitions for intelligence, drive, happiness, good, evil and so forth fell into line. Suicide, laughter, drunkenness and folly all fell inside this, too, as it computed out.

These computations stood the test of several years. And then, as you may have heard, came a war. But even wars end. Research was resumed, but now with the added necessity of applying the knowledge gained to the problems of friends who had not survived the war too well.

A researcher gets out on a rim of the unknown just so far and the guide books run out. In the libraries were thousands and thousands of mental cases, neatly recorded. *And not one case contained in it the essential data to its solution.* These cases might just as well have been written in vanishing ink for all the good they were. Beyond proving conclusively that people manifested strange mental aberrations they were worthless. How do you go about building a science of thought without being permitted to observe and without having any observed data?

Out of a multitude of personal observations in this and distant lands, it was the first task to find a constant. I had studied hypnotism in Asia. I knew hypnotism was, more or less, a fundamental. Whenever shamans, medicine men, exorcists or even modern psychologists go to work, they incline toward practices which are hypnotic.

But of what use is such a terrible, unpredictable variable as hypnotism. On some people it works. On most it doesn't. On those on whom it works it sometimes achieves good results, sometimes bad. Wild stuff, hypnotism.

The physical scientist, however, is not unacquainted with the use of a wild variable. Such erratic things usually hide real, important laws. Hypnotism was a sort of constant thread through all the cults—or hypnotic practices—but perhaps one might at least look at it.

So hypnotism was examined. A wild radical. The reason it was wild might be a good answer. The first investigation of it was quite brief. It did not need to be longer.

Examine a post-hypnotic suggestion. Patient in amnesia trance. Tell him that when he awakens he will remove his left shoe and put it on the mantel. Then tell him that he will forget he has been told and wake him up. He awakens, blinks for a while and then puts his foot forward and removes his shoe. Ask him why. "My foot's too hot." He puts the shoe on the mantel. Why? "I hate to put on a damp shoe. Warmer up here and it will dry." Keep this in mind, this experiment. The full reason for its importance did not appear for nine years. But it was recognized that, with various suggestions, one could create the appearance of various neuroses, psychoses, compulsions and repressions listed by the psychiatrist. The examination promptly went no further. One had too few answers yet. But it was clear, that *hypnotism and insanity were, somehow, identities.* A search was begun for the reason why.

For a long time and with many, many people attempts were made to unlock the riddle. What caused hypnotism? What did it do? Why did it

Dianetics:

behave unpredictably?

Examination was made of hypno-analysis. It sounds good in the texts but it doesn't work. It doesn't work for several reasons, first among them being that you can't hypnotize everybody. Further it works only occasionally, even when a person can be hypnotized. So hypno-analysis was buried along with the water-cure of Bedlam and the pre-frontal lobotomy and the demon-extraction techniques of the shamans of British Guiana, and the search for the key which could restore a mind to normal was continued.

But hypnotism wouldn't stay quite dead. Narco-synthesis* seemed a good lead, until some cases were discovered which had been "cured" by narco-synthesis. They were re-worked with the technique just to discover what had occurred. Narco-synthesis sometimes seemed to fix a man up so his war neurosis could rise to even greater heights at some future date. No, that is not entirely fair. It produces slightly higher results than a magic healing crystal in the hands of an Australian medicine man. It seemed

Narco-synthesis: the practice of inducing sleep with drugs and then talking to the patient to draw out buried thoughts.

to do something beyond what it was supposed to do, and that something beyond was bad. Here was another wild variable, a piece of the puzzle of insanity's cause. We knew WHAT Man was doing. He was surviving. Somehow, some way, he occasionally became irrational. Where did hypnotism fit into this? Why did drug hypnotism affect people so adversely at times?

These people one met and worked with did seem to be trapped somehow by something which modern methods almost never touched. And why did whole nations rise up to slaughter nations? And why did religious zealots carry a banner and crescent across three-quarters of Europe? People behave as if they'd been cursed by something. Were they basically evil? Was social training a thin veneer? Was the evil curse a natural inheritance from the tooth and claw animal kingdom? Was the brain *ever* capable of rationality? Hypnotism and narco-synthesis, unpredictable radicals, refused for a time to divulge answers.

Out of orbit again and without tools with which to work, it was necessary to hark back to the techniques of the Kayan Shaman of Borneo, amongst others. Their theory is crude; they exorcise demons. All right. We postulated that Man is evil, that the evil is native. Then we ought to be able to increase the civilized veneer by planting in him more civilization, using hypnotism. So the patient usually gets worse. That postulate didn't work. Provisionally, let's try the postulate that Man is good and follow its conclusions. And we suppose something such as the Borneo shaman's *Toh* has entered into him which directs him to do evil things.

Man has believed longer that demons inhabit men than Man has believed they did not. We assume demons. We look for some demons, one way or another. *And we found some!*

This was a discovery almost as mad as some of the patients on hand. But the thing to do was try to measure and classify demons.

Strange work for an engineer and mathematician! But it was found that the "demons" could be classified. There were several "demons" in each patient, but there were only a few classes of "demons". There were audio demons, sub-audio demons, visio demons, interior demons, exterior demons, ordering demons, directing demons, critical demons, apathetic demons, angry demons, bored demons and "curtain" demons who merely occluded things. The last seemed the most common. Looking into a few minds established soon that it was difficult to find anyone who didn't have some of these demons.

It was necessary to set up an optimum brain. That brain would be postulated, subject to change. It would be the combined best qualities of all brains studied. It would be able to visualize in color and hear with all tones and sounds present, all memories necessary to thought. It would think without talking to itself, thinking in concepts and conclusions rather than words. It would be able to imagine visually in color anything it cared to imagine and hear anything it cared to imagine it would hear. It was discovered eventually that it could also imagine smells and tactiles but this did not enter into the original. Finally it would know when it was recalling and know when it was imagining.

Now, for purposes of analogy it was necessary to go back to the electronic computer idea conceived in 1938. Circuits were drawn up for the visio and audio recall, for color and tone recall, for imagination visio and audio creation and color and tone creation. Then were drawn the memory bank circuits. All this was fairly easy at this time since some extensive work had been done on this in the thirties.

With this diagram, further circuits were set up. The optimum brain was a plain circuit. To this were added the "demon" circuits. It was found that by very ordinary electronics one could install every kind of a "demon" that had been observed.

The "demons", since none of them consented to present themselves for a proper examination as demons, were, it was concluded, installed in the brain in the same way one would install a new circuit in the optimum brain. But as there was just so much brain, it was obvious that these electronic "demons" were using parts of the optimum brain and that they were no more competent than the optimum brain inherently was. This was more postulating. All one wanted was a good result. If this hadn't worked something else would have been tried.

Thus the solution was entered upon. While the human brain is a shade too wonderful an instrument to be classified with anything as clumsy as contemporary electronics, as marvelous as modern electronics are, the analogy stands. It stands as an analogy. The whole science would hang together brightly now without that analogy. But it serves in this place.

There are no demons. No ghosts and ghouls or *Tohs*. But there are aberrative circuits. So it was reasoned. It was a postulate. And then it became something more.

One day a patient fell asleep. When he awakened he was found to be "somebody else". As "somebody else" he was questioned very carefully. This patient, as "himself", had a sonic memory block, an audio memory block, and was color-blind. He was very nervous ordinarily. Just now, awakened into being "somebody else" he was calm. He spoke in a lower voice tone. Here, obviously, one was confronting one of these electronic screw-ups the savants call schizophrenics. But not so. This was the basic personality of the patient himself, possessed of an optimum brain!

It was very rapidly established that he had color-visio recall on anything, tone-audio recall, tone-audio and color-visio imagination and entire co-ordinative control. He knew when he was imagining and when he was recalling and that, too, was something he had not been able to do before.

He wanted to know something. He wanted to know when the operator was going to help him get himself squared around. He had a lot of things to do. He wanted to help his wife out so she wouldn't have to support the family. How unlike the patient of an hour before!

He obligingly did some mental computations with accuracy and clarity and then he was permitted to lie down and sleep. He woke up with no recollection of what had happened. He had his old symptoms. Nothing could shake those electronic blocks. He didn't even know if he had eaten lunch, the color of my scarf, and as for his wife, served her right for being a condemned woman.

This was a first introduction to basic personality. It was a long way from a last acquaintance. It was found that it was possible to contact optimum brain operation in a number of people.

And the basic personalities contacted were invariably strong, hardy, and constructively good! They were the same personalities as the patients had in a normal state minus certain mental powers, plus electronic demons and plus general unhappiness. I found that a "hardened criminal" with an obvious "criminal mind" was, in basic personality, a sincere, intelligent being with ambition and cooperativeness.

This was incredible. If this was basic brain, then basic brain was good. Then Man was basically good. Social nature was inherent! If this was basic brain—

It was. That is a "clear". But we pull ahead of the story.

People were uniformly miserable being aberrated. The most miserable patient on the rolls had an aberration that made her act "happy" and the most nervous aberree one would ever care to encounter had a mastering aberration about being always "calm". She said she was happy and tried to make herself and everyone believe it. He said he was calm. He instantly flew into a nervous fit if you told him he wasn't calm.

Tentatively and cautiously a conclusion was drawn that the optimum brain is the unaberrated brain, that the optimum brain is also the basic personality, that the basic personality, unless organically deranged, was good. If Man were basically good, then only a "black enchantment" could make him evil.

What was the source of this enchantment?

Did we admit superstitions and demons as actualities and suppose the source was something weird and wonderful in the way of ectoplasm? Or did we part company with many current beliefs and become something a little more scientific?

The source, then, must be the exterior world. A basic personality, so anxious to be strong, probably would not aberrate itself without some very powerful internal personal devil at work. But with the devils and "things that go boomp in the night" heaved into the scrap heap, what did we have left? There was the exterior world and only the exterior world.

Good enough: we'll see if this works again. Somehow the exterior world gets interior. The individual becomes possessed of some unknowns which set up circuits against his consent, the individual is aberrated, and is less able to survive.

The next hunt was for the unknown factor. The track looked pretty fair, so far, but the idea was to formulate a science, of thought. And a science, at least to an engineer, is something pretty precise. It had to be built on axioms to which there are precious few, if any, exceptions. It has to produce predictable results uniformly and *every time*.

Perhaps engineering sciences are this way because natural obstacles oppose the engineer, and matter has a rather unhandy way of refusing to be overlooked because someone has an opinion. If an engineer forms an opinion that trains can run in thin air and so omits the construction of a bridge across a stream, gravity is going to take over and spill one train into one stream.

Thus, if we are to have a science of thought, it is going to be necessary to have workable axioms which, applied with techniques, will produce uniform results in all cases and produce them invariably.

A great deal of compartmentation of the problems had already been done, as previously mentioned or in the course of the work. This was necessary in order to examine the problem proper which was Man in the Universe.

First we divided what we could probably think about and had to think about from what we probably didn't have to think about, for purposes of our solution. Next we had to think about all men. Then a few men. Finally the individual man and at last a portion of the aberrative pattern of an individual man.

How did the exterior world become an interior aberration?

There were many false starts and blind passages just as there had been in determining what an optimum brain would be. There were still so many variables and possible erroneous combinations in the computation that it looked like something out of Kant. But there is no argument with results. There is no substitute for a bridge heavy enough to hold a train.

I tried, on the off-chance that they might be right, several schools of psychology—Jung, Adler. Even Freud. But not very seriously because over half the patients on the rolls had been given very extensive courses in psychoanalysis by experts, with no great results. The work of Pavlov was reviewed in case there was something there. But men aren't dogs. Looking back on these people's work now, a lot of things they did made sense. But reading their work and using it when one did *not* know, they didn't make sense, from which can be concluded that rear-view mirrors six feet wide tell more to a man

34

who is driving with a peephole in front than he knew when he was approaching an object.

Then came up another of a multitude of the doctrines which had to be originated to resolve this work. *The selection of importances.* One looked at a sea of facts. Every drop in the sea is like every other drop. Some few of the drops are of vast importance. How to find one? How to tell when it is important? A lot of prior art in the field of the mind—and as far as I was concerned, all of it—is like that. Ten thousand facts, all and each with one apparent unit importance value. Now, unerringly select the right one. Yes, once one has found, by some other means, the right one, it is very simple to look over the facts and pick out the proper one and say, "See? There it was all the time. Old Whoosis knew what he was doing." But try it before you know! It's a cinch Old Whoosis did not know or he would have red-tabbed the fact and thrown the others away. So, with this new doctrine of the selection of importances, all data not of personal testing or discovery was jettisoned. I had been led up so many blind alleys by unthorough observation and careless work on the part of forerunners in this business that it was time to decide that it was much, much easier to construct a whole premise than it was to go needle-in-thehaystacking. It was a rather desperate turn of affairs when this came about. Nothing was working. I found I had imbibed, unconsciously, a lot of prior errors which were impeding the project. There were literally hundreds of these "why everybody knows that"—which had no more foundation in experimentation or observation than a Roman omen.

So it was concluded that the exterior world got interior through some process entirely unknown and unsuspected. There was memory. How much did we know about memory? How many kinds of memory might there be? How many banks was the nervous system running on? The problem was not *where* they were. That was an off-track problem. The problem was *what* they were.

I drew up some fancy schematics, threw them away and drew some more. I drew up a genetic bank, a mimic bank, a social bank, a scientific bank. But they were all wrong. They couldn't be located in a brain as such.

Then a terrible thought came. There was this doctrine of the selection of importances. But there was another, earlier doctrine—the introduction of an arbitrary. Introduce an arbitrary and if it is only an arbitrary, the whole computation goes out. What was I doing that had introduced an arbitrary? Was there another "why, everybody knows that—" still in this computation?

It's hard to make your wits kick out things which have been accepted, unquestioned, from earliest childhood, hard to suspect them. Another sea of facts, and these in the memory bank of the computer trying to find them.

There was an arbitrary. Who introduced it I don't know but it was probably about the third shaman who practiced shortly after the third generation of talking men had begun to talk.

Mind *and* body.

There's the pleasant little hooker. Take a good look at it. Mind AND body. This is one of those things like a ghost. Somebody said they saw one. They don't recall just who it was or where but they're *sure—*

Who said they were separate? Where's the evidence? Everybody who has measured a mind without the body being present please raise both his hands. Oh, yes, sure. In books. I'm talking to you but I'm not there in the room with you right now. So mind is naturally separate from body. Only it isn't. A man's body can leave footprints. Those are products of the body. The products of the mind can also be viewed when the body is not there, but these are *products of* and the product of the object is not the object.

There *can* be a mind without a body—*but* we must not confuse the products of the mind with the mind itself.

So let's consider these mental products and the body as a unity. Then the body remembers. It may co-ordinate its activities in a mechanism called the brain, but the fact is that the brain is also part of the nervous system and the nervous system extends all through the body. If you don't believe it, pinch yourself. Then wait ten minutes and go back to the time you pinched yourself. Time travel back. Pretend you are all back there. You will feel the pinch; that's memory.

All right. If the body remembers and if the mind and body are not necessarily two items, then what memories would be the strongest? Why, memories that have pain in them, of course. And then what memories would be the strongest? Those which would have the most physical pain. But these are not recallable!

Maybe it's the wrong postulate, maybe people are in fifty pieces not just one, but let's try it on for size.

So I pinched a few patients and made them pretend they had moved back to the moment of the pinch. And it hurt them again. And one young man, who cared a great deal about science and not much about his physical being, volunteered for a nice, heavy knockout.

And I took him back to it and he recalled it.

Then came the idea that maybe people remembered their operations. And so a technique was invented and the next thing I knew I had a memory of a nitrous oxide dental operation laid wide open and in recall, complete with pain.

A great deal of experimentation and observation disclosed the fact that there were no moments of "unconsciousness". And that was another misconception which had held up Man's progress.

Dianetics:

"Unconsciousness". Some day the word will either be gone or have a new meaning because just now it doesn't really mean a thing.

The *unconscious mind* is the mind which is *always conscious*. So there is no "unconscious mind". And there is no "unconsciousness". This made modern psychology look like Tarawa after the marines had landed; for this is about as easy to prove as the statement that when an apple is held three feet in the air and let fall, it drops, conditions being normal.

It was necessary, then, to redraw all the circuit diagrams and to bring forth some terminology which would not be quite as erroneous as "unconsciousness" and "the unconscious mind".

For handy purposes, in view of the fact that I had got myself into difficulties before by using words with accepted meanings, I turned some adjectives into nouns, scrambled a few syllables and tried to get as far as possible from the focus of infection: Authority. By using old terms, one interposes, in communication, the necessity of explaining away an old meaning before he can explain the new one. A whole chain of thought can get thoroughly jammed up in trying to explain that while this word meant . . .

it now means ... Usually, in communications, one is not permitted to get beyond an effort to explain one does not mean ...

Now there is no reason here to go into an evolution of terms in Dianetics. The cycle of the evolution is not yet complete. And so I will place here terms which were long afterwards conceived. They are not yet stet. But their definitions are not quibbles: the order of definition is clear in the order of apples are apples.

The important thing is what we are defining. There were several heuristic principles on which the initial work was based which were "understood". One was that the human mind was capable of solving some of the riddles of existence. At this stage in the evolution of Dianetics, after "unconsciousness" had been smoked out of the "why, everybody knows that—" class of information and labeled for what it was, an error, it was necessary to look over some of the "understood" postulates of 1938. And one of those "everybody knows" postulates had been that the human mind is not capable of understanding the workings of the human mind.

And "everybody knew that" the human mind was

41

liable to err, that it was stupid, and was very easily aberrated by such small things as because papa loved mama and Jimmy wanted to love mama too.

And "everybody knew that" the workings of the human mind were enormously complex; so involved that a complete direct solution of the problem was impossible. That, in effect, the human mind was a Rube Goldberg* device built up of an enormously unstable and delicately balanced pile of odd-shaped bits of emotion and experience, liable to collapse at any time.

From the engineering viewpoint, that seems a little strange. Two billion years of evolution, a billion successive test models, would tend to produce a fairly streamlined, functional mechanism. After that much experience, animal life would be expected to produce a truly functional mechanism—and Rube Goldberg's devices are amusing because they are so insanely non-functional. It somehow doesn't seem probable that two billion years of trial and error development could wind up with a clumsy, complex, poorly balanced mechanism for survival—and that jerry-

*American cartoonist.

built thing an absolute master of all other animal life!

Some of those "everybody knows that—" postulates needed checking—and checking out of the computation.

First, everybody knows that "to err is human". And second, everybody knows that we are pawns in the hairy grasp of some ogre who is and always will be unknown.

Only this didn't sound like engineering to me. I'd listened to the voodoo drums in Cap Haitien and the bullhorns in the lama temples of the Western Hills. The people who beat those drums and blew those horns were subject to disease, starvation and terror. Looked like we had a ratio at work here. The closer a civilization—or a man—moved toward admitting the ability of the human mind to compute—the closer the proposition was entered that natural obstacles and chaos were susceptible to orderly solution—the better he—or they—fared in the business of living. And here we were back with our original postulate again, SURVIVE! Now this computation would be warranted only if it worked.

Dianetics:

But it was a not unwarrantable conclusion. I had had experience now with basic personality. Basic personality could compute like a well greased Univac. It was constructive. It was rational. It was sane.

And so we entered upon the next seven league boot stride in this evolution. What was sanity? It was rationality. A man was sane in the ratio that he could compute accurately, limited only by information and viewpoint.

What was the optimum brain? It was an entirely rational brain. What did one have to have to be entirely rational? What would any electronic computer have to have? All data must be available for inspection. All data it contained must be derived from its own computation or it must be able to compute and check the data it is fed. Take any electronic calculator . . . no, on second thought, don't take them. They're not smart enough to be on the same plane with the mind because they are of a greatly sub order of magnitude. Very well, let's take the mind itself, the optimum mind. Compare it to itself. When did Man become sentient? It's not absolutely necessary to the problem or these results to know just when or where Man began to THINK,

44

but let's compare him to his fellow mammals. What does he have that the other mammals don't have? What can he do that they can't do? What does he have that they have?

All it takes is the right question. What does he have that they have? He does have something—and he has something more than they have. Is it the same order? More or less.

You never met a dog yet that could drive a car, or a rat that could do arithmetic. But you have men that couldn't drive a car, and men that couldn't do much better arithmetic than a rat. How did such men vary from the average?

It seemed that the average man had a computer that was not only better, it was infinitely finer than any animal's brain. When something happens to the computer, Man is no longer MAN but a dog or a rat, for purposes of comparison in mental power.

Man's computer must be pretty good. After all those millions of years of evolution, it should be—in fact it should, by this time, have evolved a perfect computer, one that didn't give wrong answers because it couldn't make a mistake. We've already

developed electronic computing machines so designed, with such built-in self-checking circuits, that
they *can't* by their very nature, turn out a wrong
answer. Those machines stop themselves and sum-
mon an operator if something goes wrong so that the
computer starts producing a wrong answer. We know
how to make a machine that would not only do that,
but set up circuits to find the error, and correct the
erring circuit. If men have figured out ways to do
that with a machine already—

I had long since laid aside the idea that one
could do this job by dissecting a neurone. Dead,
they don't talk. Now I had to lay aside the idea
that the brain's structural mechanism could even
be guessed at this stage. But working on the
heuristic basis of what works, it is not necessary to
know *how* it is done in terms of physical mechanism if we can show that it *is* done. It was
convenient to use electronic circuits as analogs, and
the analogy of an electronic brain, because I knew
the terms of these things. The brain may or may
not run on electric currents; what things can be
measured in and around it by voltmeters are
interesting. But electricity itself is measured indi-
rectly today. Temperature is measured by the
coefficient of expansion caused by temperature.

Encephalographs* are useful working around a brain but that doesn't mean that the brain is as clumsy and crude as a vacuum tube rig. This was a necessary step because if the problem were to be solved one had to suppose that the brain could be patched up and with some method decidedly short of surgery.

So here was what I seemed to be working with: a computing machine that could work from data stored in memory banks, and was so designed that the computer circuits themselves were inherently incapable of miscomputation. The computer was equipped with sensing devices—the sensory organs— which enabled it to compare its conclusions with the external world, and thus to use the data of the external world as part of the checking feedback circuits. If the derived answer did not match the observed external world, since the computing circuits were inherently incapable of producing a wrong computation, the data used in the problem must itself be wrong. Thus, a perfect, errorless computer can use external world data to check the validity of and evaluate its own data input. *Only* if the computational mechanism is inherently error-

---

Encephalograph: an apparatus for detecting and recording brain waves.

proof would this be possible. But men have already figured out mechanically simple ways of making an error-proof computer—and if Man can figure it out at this stage of the game, two billion years of evolution could and would.

How did the mind work? Well, to solve this problem we did not have to know. Dr. Shannon commented that he had tried every way he could think of to compute the material in the memory bank of the brain, and he had been forced to conclude that the brain could not retain more than three months' worth of observations if it recorded everything. And Dianetic research reveals that everything is recorded and retained. Dr. McCulloch of the University of Illinois postulating the electronic brain in 1949 is said to have done some computation to the effect that if the human brain cost a million dollars to build, its vacuum tubes would have to cost about 0.1 cent each, that the amount of power it would consume would light New York City and that it would take Niagara Falls to cool it. To these competent gentlemen we deliver up the problems of structure. To date Dianetics has not violated anything actually known about structure. Indeed, by studious application of Dianetic principles, maybe the problem of structure can be better approached.

48

But at a swoop, we have all this off our minds. We are dealing with function and ability and the adjustment of that function to the end of obtaining maximum operation. And we are dealing with an inherently *perfect* calculator.

We are dealing with a calculator which runs entirely on the principle that it must be right and must find out why if it isn't right. Its code might be stated as, "And I pledge myself to be right first, last and always and to be nothing but right and never to be, under any circumstances, wrong."

Now this is what you would expect of an organ dedicated to computing a life and death matter like survival. If you or I were building a calculator, we'd build one that would always give correct answers. Now, if the calculator we built was also itself, a personality, it would maintain that it was right as well.

Having observed this computer in its optimum state as the basic personality, the conclusion was very far from a mere postulate. And so we call this computer the "analytical mind". We could subdivide things further and get complicated by saying that there is an "I" as well as a computer, but this leads off in another direction. And so the "analytical mind" or the "analyzer" is a computer and the "I" for our purposes. All we want is a good *workable solution.*

The next thing we must consider is what apparently makes Man a sentient being and that consideration leads us into the conclusion that possession of this analyzer raises Man far above his fellow mammals. For as long as Man is rational, he is superior. When that rationality reduces, so does his state of being. So it can be postulated that it is this analyzer which places the gap between a dog and a man.

Study of animals has long been popular with experimental psychologists, but they must not be mis-evaluated. Pavlov's work was interesting: it proved dogs will be dogs. Now by light of these new observations and deductions it proved more than Pavlov knew. It proved men *weren't* dogs. Must be an answer here somewhere. Let's see. I've trained a lot of dogs. I've also trained a lot of kids. Once I had a theory that if you trained a kid as patiently as you trained a dog, then you would have an obedient kid. Didn't work. Hm-m-m. That's right. It didn't work. The more calmly and patiently one tried to make that kid into a well-trained dog—"Come here" and he'd run away—hm-m-m. Must be some difference between kids and dogs. Well, what do dogs have that kids don't have? Mentally, probably nothing. But what do kids have that dogs don't have? A good analytical mind!

Let us then observe this human analytical mind more closely. It must have a characteristic dissimilar to animal minds—minds in lower orders of mammals. We postulate that this characteristic must have a high survival value, it is evidently so prominent and widespread and the analyzer—hm-m-m.

The analyzer must have some quality which makes it a slightly different thinking apparatus than those observed in rats and dogs. Not just sensitivity and complexity. Must have something newer and better. Another principle? Well hardly a whole principle but—

The more rational the mind, the more sane the man. The less rational the mind, the closer Man approaches in conduct his cousins of the mammalian family. What makes the mind irrational?

I set up a series of experiments, using the basic personalities I could contact above or below the level of the aberrated personalities and in these confirmed the clarity and optimum performance of the basic computer. Some of these patients were quite aberrated until they were in an hypnotic amnesia trance at which time they could be freed of operator control. The aberrations were not present. Stutterers did not stutter. Harlots became moral. Arithmetic was easy. Color-visio, tone-audio recall. Color-visio, tone-audio imagination. Knowledge of what was imagination and what wasn't. The "demons" had got parked somewhere. The circuits and filters causing aberration had been by-passed, to be more precisely technical and scientific.

Now let's postulate that the aberrative circuits have been somehow introduced from the external world—covered that ground pretty well, pretty solid ground.

And here's an answer. The introduced by-pass circuits and filters became the aberrations in some way we did not yet understand. And what new complexion did this give the analyzer?

Further research tended to indicate that the answer might be contained in the term "determinism". A careful inspection of this computation confirmed observations. Nothing was violated. Did it work?

Let's postulate this perfect computer. It is *responsible*. It has to be responsible. It is *right*. It has to be right. What would make it wrong? Exterior determinism beyond its capacity to reject. *If it could not kick out a false datum it would have to compute with it.* Then, and only then, would the perfect computer get wrong answers. A perfect computer had to be *self*-determined within the limits of necessary efforts to solve a problem. No self-determinism, bad computation.

The machine had to be in a large measure *self-determined* or it would not work. That was the conclusion. Good or bad, did it lead to further results?

It did.

When exterior determinism was entered into a human being so as to overbalance his self-determinism the correctness of his solutions fell off rapidly.

Let's take any common adding machine. We put

into it the order that all of its solutions must contain the figure 7. We hold down 7 and put on the computer the problem of 6 x 1. The answer is wrong. But we still hold down 7. To all intents and purposes here, that machine is crazy. Why? Because it won't compute accurately so long as 7 is held down. Now we release 7 and put a very large problem on the machine and get a correct answer. The machine is now sane—rational. It gives correct answers. On an electronic computer we short the 7 so it is always added in, no matter what keys are punched. Then we give the machine to a storekeeper. He tries to use it and throws it on the junk heap because it won't give correct answers and he doesn't know anything about troubleshooting electronics and cares less. All he wants is a correct total.

Admitting the analytical mind computation, and admitting it only so long as it works, where does it get a held-down 7—an enforced wrong datum?

Now a computer is not necessarily its memory bank. Memory banks can be added and detached to a standard computer of the electronic type. Where do we look for the error? Is it in the memory bank?

The search for what was holding down 7 involved

quite a little hard work and speculation and guesses. Some more work had to be done on the computer—the analytical mind. And then came what seemed to be a bright thought. Supposing we set up the whole computer as the demon. A demon that is always and invariably right. Let's install one in a brain so that the computer can project outside the body and give the body orders. Let's make the computer a circuit independent of the individual. Well, hypnotism has some uses. Good tool for research sometimes even if it is a prime villain in aberration.

Two things happened the moment this was done. The computer could direct the body as an "exterior entity" and draw on the memory banks at will for anything. *Seven was no longer held down.*

Naturally this was a freak test, one that could be set up only in an excellent hypnotic patient. And it could be installed only as a temporary thing.

This artificial demon knew *everything*. The patient could hear him when the patient was awake. The demon was gifted with perfect recall. He directed the patient admirably. He did computations by moving the patient's hand—automatic writing—and he did things the patient evidently could not do.

But why could it? We had artificially split the analyzer away from the aberrated patient, making a new by-pass circuit which by-passed all the aberrated circuits. This would have been a wonderful solution if it had not been for the fact that the patient was soon a slave to the demon and that the control, after a while, began to pick up aberrations out of the plentiful store the patient had. But it served to test the memory banks.

Something must be wrong about these banks. Everything else was in good order. The banks contained an infinity of data which appalled one in its very completeness. So there ensued a good, long search to find something awry in the banks. In amnesia sleep or under narco-synthesis, the banks could be very thoroughly ransacked. By automatic writing, speaking and clairvoyance they could be further tapped.

This was a mad sort of way to go about things. But once one started to investigate memory banks, so much data kept turning up that he had to continue.

There's no place here for a recital of everything that was found in the human memory bank, its completeness, exactness and minuteness or its fantastically complicated, but very smart cross-filing system. But a resume is necessary of some high points.

In the first place the banks contain a complete color-video record of a person's whole life, no matter the "demon" circuits. The last occlude or falsify. They do not alter the bank or the accuracy of the bank. A "poor" memory means a curtained memory, the memory being complete. *Every perception observed in a lifetime is to be found in the banks.* All the perceptions. In good order.

Memories are filed by time. They have an age and emotional label, a state of physical being label, and a precise and exhaustive record of everything perceived by organic sensation, smell, taste, tactile, audio and visio perceptics *plus* the train of thought of the analyzer of that moment.

There is no inaccuracy in the banks. Inaccuracy can, of course, be caused by surgery or injury involving actually removed portions. Electric shock and other psychiatric efforts are equivocal. Prefrontal lobotomy is such certain and complete mind-murder that one cannot be certain thereafter

Dianetics:

of anything in the patient except zombiism.

Anyway, the memory banks are so fantastically complete and in such good order behind the by-pass circuits in any man not organically tampered with, that I very nearly wore out the rug trying to conceive it. Very well, there was something between the banks and the analyzer. Must be. The banks were complete. The circuits were intact. In any patient organically sound, and that includes all patients who have psychosomatic ills—the basic personality was apparently intact, the banks were intact. But the banks and the analyzer somehow did not track.

Well, let's take another look. This is an engineering problem. So far it has surrendered beautifully to engineering thought and computation. Apparently it should go right on surrendering. But let's look at Freud. There's his Censor. Let's see if there's a censor between the banks and the analyzer.

That folded up in about two seconds max. The censor is a composite of by-pass circuits and is about as natural and necessary to a human being as the fifth wheel on a motorcycle. There isn't any censor. Served me right for trying to lean on Authority. In terms of authority, if you can spell it, it's right. In terms of engineering, if it can't be found and measured in some fashion, it's probably absent.

I rechecked the memory banks. How was I withdrawing data? I was using automatic writing for some, by-pass circuit for others, direct regression and revivification on the old line Hindu principle for others. I set about trying to classify what kind of data I was getting with each method of recall. All of a sudden the problem fell apart. By automatic writing I was getting data not available to the analyzer. By by-pass I was getting data not available otherwise. By regression and revivification material was being procured only a little better than could be recalled by the tranced subject. The data I could check was found to be invariably accurate by any of these methods. What was the difference between automatic writing data and simple trance data?

I took a patient's automatic data and regressed him to its period. He could not recall it. The data concerned a broken leg and a hospital. I bucked him into the incident by main force.

The patient received a very sharp pain in the area of the old break.

Dianetics:

This was a long way from hypno-analysis. This was an effort to find an interposition between memory banks and analyzer, not an effort to relieve "traumatic experiences".

And there was the answer. Why not? Very simple. It had been sitting right there staring at me since 1938. Oh, these six-foot wide rear view mirrors! I had even made a law about it.

The function of the mind included the avoidance of pain. Pain was unsurvival. Avoid it.

And that's it—the way to hold down seven! You can hold it down with physical pain! The exterior world enters into the man and becomes memory bank. The analyzer uses memory bank. The analyzer uses the exterior world. The analyzer is caught between yesterday's exterior world now interior and today and tomorrow's exterior world, still exterior.

Can it just be that this analyzer gets its data on one perceptic circuit? Can it be that that perceptic circuit carries yesterday and today both? Well, however that may be, the analyzer certainly behaves to yesterday's interior world the same way it behaves to today's exterior world so far as the avoidance of pain goes. The law works both ways.

The analyzer avoids yesterday's pain as well as today's pain. Well, that's reasonable. If you avoid yesterday's pain in today's environment, you have a much better chance to survive. In fact—But see here, there's more to the problem than this. If the analyzer had a clear view of yesterday's pain it could better avoid it in today. That would be good operation.

That was the "flaw" in the machine. But it was a highly necessary "flaw". Just because an organism is built to survive, molded to survive and intended to survive does not mean that it will, as a matter of course, be perfect.

But the analyzer *was* perfect.

The banks were perfect.

The analyzer just plain wouldn't ever let the irrationalities of exterior world inside as long as it could help it.

As long as it could help it!

I was probing now for the villain of the piece. He

was not found for a while. Many experiments were made. Efforts were made to make several patients well by simply breaking through the pain wall the analyzer was "seeking to avoid". A lot of painful incidents were broken, mental and physical anguish by the library full, and without much relief. The patients relapsed.

Then it was discovered that when a patient was bucked through a period when he was "unconscious", he showed some improvement. Then it was discovered that these "unconscious" periods were rather like periods of hypnosis driven home by pain. The patient responded as though the "unconscious period" had been post-hypnotic suggestion!

From this series of experiments a prime datum was picked up.

You relieve the pain and the "unconsciousness" and the suggestive power goes away. The subject did not have to have any of the mumbo jumbo of hypnosis in this "unconscious period". But every perceptic perceived tended to aberrate him.

I did not realize until then that I was playing tag with a hitherto unappreciated mid-evolution step in

Man. If he was once a polliwog, he had never lost any of the parts he had evolved through. How does a fish think?

Well, let's see how a fish would respond to pain. He is swimming in brackish water of yellow color over a green bottom, tasting shrimp. A big fish hits him a whack, but does not kill him. Our fish lives to come back another day. This time he swims into an area of brackish water with a black bottom. He gets a little nervous. Then the water becomes a yellow color. The fish becomes very, very alert. He coasts along and gets over a green bottom. Then he tastes shrimp and instantly swims away at a terrific rate.

Now, what if Man still had his lower organism responses? Well, it seemed, on experiment, that he did. Drug him with ether and hurt him. Then give him a whiff of ether and he gets nervous. Start to put him out and he begins to fight. Other experiments all gave the same conclusion.

Lower organisms can be precisely and predictably determined in their responses. Pavlov's dog. Any dog you ever trained. The dog may have something of an analyzer too, but he is a pushbutton animal. And so is Man. Ah, yes, so is Man. You know, just like rats.

Dianetics:

Only Man *isn't!* Man has a wide power of choice. Interfere with that wide power and there's trouble brewing. Aberrate him enough and he's unpredictably pushbuttonable. Cut his brain out with a knife—and he can be trained to speak woof-woof for his food. But by golly, you better cut pretty well to get a good, satisfactory one hundred percent of the time woof-woof!

What happens when a man gets "knocked out"? He "isn't there". *But all the memory recordings during the period are.* What happens when you knock him half out? He does strange, automatic things. What happens when his analyzer is so aberrated that ... hey! Wait! How would you build a good, sensitive analyzer? Would you leave it connected to every shock? Huhuh! You'd fuse it so it would live to think another day. In an emergency what kind of a response do you want? Automatic!

Stove hot, hand on stove, withdraw hand. Do you do a computation on that? No indeed. What withdrew the hand? The analyzer? No. What happened to the analyzer for an instant during the shock? The analyzer goes out of circuit and leaves a mechanical determining director in full charge! A good, fast identity-thinking director.

The analyzer does not think in identities. It thinks in differences, similarities. When it loses its power to differentiate and thinks in identities—no, it never does that. That's madness and the analyzer does *not* go mad. But something around here thinks in identities. Start working on a patient and find out that hash equals snow equals an ache in the knee—that's identity thinking.

We don't know here what really happens to that analyzer. But we do know that we have found something which interposes between the banks and the computer. Something which thinks in identities, has a high priority over reason during moments of stress, can be found whenever a man is sent into some of yesterday's unconscious moments.

We know what it does now. It takes command when the analyzer is out of circuit. Whether or not it is the old style mind which Man did not shed while graduating to sentience by developing an analyzer is beside the point. Whether or not it is a structural entity of a combination of "unconscious periods" is equally outside our concern here. We are working in function and we want answers that work every time.

Call this the *reactive mind*. It is a mind which is

constructed to work in moments of enormous physical pain. It is rugged. It works all the way down to the bottom and within a millimeter of death. Maybe it's almost impossible to build a sharply sentient mind which would operate under the terrible conditions of agony in which we find the reactive mind operating. Maybe the reactive mind . . . well, that's structure. Here it is as function.

The reactive mind thinks in identities. It is a stimulus-response mind. Its actions are exteriorly determined. It has no power of choice. It puts physical pain data forward during moments of physical pain in an effort to save the organism. So long as its mandates and commands are obeyed it withholds the physical pain. As soon as the organism starts to go against its commands, it inflicts the pain.

The fish, had he failed to swim away when in a danger area where he had been attacked, would have been forced away by the crude mechanism of pain going into restimulation. No swim equals aching side. Swim equals all right.

The analyzer blows its fuses as any good machine would when its delicate mechanism is about to be destroyed by overload. That's survival. The reactive mind kicks in when the analyzer is out. That's survival.

But something must go wrong. This was a pretty good scheme of things. But it didn't always work.

Or it worked too well.

Thus were discovered the reactive memory bank and its total contents, the engrams and their locks.

An engram is an energy-picture. It is made during a period of physical pain when the analyzer is out of circuit and the organism experiences something it conceives to be or which is contrary to survival. An engram is received only in the absence of the analytical power.

When the analyzer is out of circuit, data of high priority value can pass, without evaluation by the analyzer, into the memory bank. There it becomes a part of the emergency bank. This is a red-tab bank, the reactive mind, composed of high-priority, dangerous situations which the organism has experienced. The reactive mind has this bank as its sole source of information. The reactive mind thinks in identities with this red-tab bank. So long as the analyzer is *fully* in circuit, the red-tab bank is null and void. With the analyzer partially out of circuit—as in weariness, drunkenness, or illness—a part of this bank can cut in.

Let's begin to call "unconsciousness" a new word: ANATEN. *An*alytical *Atten*uation. There is greater or lesser anaten. A man goes under ether. He becomes anaten. He is hit in the jaw and goes anaten.

Now what does an engram contain? Clinical examination of this object of interest demonstrates that the engram consists of anaten, time, physical age, emotion, physical pain, and every percept in order of sequence. Words, sights, smells, everything that was there.

We had to organize a new sub-science here to think about engrams properly. It's the science of Perceptics. Know your general semantics?* Well, same organization, only we take in all the perceptics and we show where the meaning of each perceptic originates and why Man can't nonidentify with ease and aplomb so long as he has engrams.

General Semantics: a study of meaning (semantics) stressing the distinction between words and objects.

The automatic writing I was getting was straight out of engrams. That and by-pass circuits would disclose data received during anaten—engrams. And then I discovered that these engrams had a peculiar faculty. They could create their own circuits, parasitically using the host circuits.

Here's how an engram can be established: Mary, age 2, knocked out by dog, dog bites. Content of engram: anaten; age 2 (physical structure); smell of environment and dog; sight of dog jaws gaping and white teeth; organic sensation of pain in back of head (hit pavement); pain in posterior; dog bite in cheek; tactile of dog fur, concrete (elbows on pavement), hot dog breath; emotion; physical pain plus endocrine response; audio of dog growl and passing car.

What Mary does with the engram: she does not "remember" the incident but sometimes plays she is a dog jumping on people and biting them. Otherwise no reaction. Then, at age 10 similar circumstances, no great anaten, the engram is restimulated. After this she has headaches when dogs bark or when cars pass that sound like *that* car, but only responds to the engram when she is tired or harassed otherwise. The engram was first dormant—data waiting just in

Dianetics:

case. Next it was keyed in*—stuff we have to watch out for. Then it was thereafter restimulated whenever any combination of its perceptics appeared while Mary was in slight anaten (weary). When forty years of age she responded in exactly the same way, and still had not the slightest conscious understanding of the real reason!

Now let's consider what would have happened if Mary's mama had yelled something really choice: "Be calm! Be calm! Oh, my darling, it's always this way. Get out, get out!" Something mama had tucked away as the proper thing to do and say when dogs bite daughters.

We here have what amounts to a post-hypnotic suggestion: identity (equals) thought. All the perceptics equal all the words equals a dog equals mama equals get out, et cetera, et cetera, et cetera, and each equals all and any part of each. No wonder nobody could compute a madman! This is irrationality de luxe. Literally this computation of identity thought makes no sense. But it's survival data and it better be obeyed or the cheek will hurt, the head will ache and the elbows will get a permanent "dermatitis".

Keyed in: restimulated for the first time; activated.

But remember that this engram also had, as a tab, anaten, the exact degree of anaten present during that moment. The analyzer is a fine device but it is also, evidently, a physical organ, probably the pre-frontal lobes, and organic sensation includes several things. Restimulation brings about this state of affairs: "Analyzer shut-off." "Reactive mind to cells. Red-tab dog in sight. Shut off analyzer. This is a priority situation. That is all."

The degree of anaten is very far from the original in the facsimile. But it is sufficient to produce a reduced state of analyzing, in effect a reduced sanity. The subject just has a feeling of dull, stupid mental confusion many times, a sort of dumb, unreasoned and unidentified emotion that seems to stop thought in numbness. You've had it! Thus we have a situation which begins to approach a pushbutton determinism. The engram which has become keyed in can, when the individual is slightly anaten—weary, ill, sleepy—be pushbuttoned. Use the key word to the slightly anaten subject which is contained in one of his engrams and one of that engram's reactions may be observed. Push the button thoroughly enough and a full dramatization can be effected—he will *re-enact* the original situation!

71

Dianetics:

Thus the red-tab "memory" bank of the reactive mind. The discovery of this bank is one of the several original discoveries of Dianetics. Many parts of Dianetics can be found, if improperly evaluated, in old philosophic schools or in modern practice, but there remain a few entirely new facts which have no prior art. This red-tab bank is a very special affair and is quite different in composition, content and circuit from the analytical banks—conscious banks containing data which can be "remembered".

The reason this bank was never discovered before is not difficult to find. The red-tab bank content was implanted when the analyzer was out of circuit—unconscious. It is located then many strata below conscious awareness in the stupefactions of a physical knockout. When one tried to get to it with hypnotism or narco-synthesis he was confronted with a patient who simply looked knocked out, who was unresponsive to everything. As narco-synthesis and hypnotism both savor of sleep, the deeper sleep of the composite whole of all the past knockouts of a lifetime render the patient entirely insensible even when one was squarely on top of the reactive bank. So this bank remained hidden and unknown. And that is a sad thing because unless one knows about this bank the entire problem of Man's imperfection, his insanity, his wars, his unhappiness, can go begging or get into the files of a shaman or a neurosurgeon. Much more widely, the hidden character of this bank can be said to be responsible for irrational conduct on the part of all Mankind. And how many lives has that cost in the last four thousand years?

It is a very peculiar sort of a bank. It is the *only* bank in the human mind from which any content can be exhausted. All its content is pain and unconsciousness. And only physical pain can be deleted from the mind. Now wouldn't you say that this was a peculiar sort of a bank? Here it is full of experiences which, because of the way they are filed, can drive a man to suicide or other madness. Here it is with its memories all ready to click into the motor controls of the body, ready, without so much as a by-your-leave from the sentient analyzer, to make a man run insanely until he drops from heart failure. Here it is able to change the perfect structure of the body into a nightmare thing with a fetus-like face and wasted or undeveloped limbs. Here it is ready to manufacture anything you can name by way of physical ills or at least to predispose them, possibly even cancer. Here it is filling hospitals, mental institutions and jails. And yet it is the one portion of

73

human memory that can be modified and changed!

What price some of the old philosophies when the reducible "memory" is one of pain?

Try any technique you can name on a pleasant or even a merely passing memory in one of the conscious banks. It will stay right where it is, indelible, particularly the pleasurable ones. But a "memory" in the red-tab bank, when properly approached by Dianetic technique, will vanish out of that bank entirely. It refiles as a memory in the conscious level banks, and as such, by the way, is fantastically difficult to locate—on the order of what you ate for dinner on June 2nd when you were two years of age—and when found bears the tag "found to be nonsurvival data, do not permit it or similar data into any fundamental computations". And one of these unconscious "memories" when treated, produces about the same emotional response afterwards as a mildly amusing joke.

The red-tab bank could cause circuits to be set up which looked and sounded like demons. It could occlude the conscious bank in part or so thoroughly that it appeared that there was no past. It could command and order a person about like a moron might control a robot. And yet it is perishable. And it can be de-intensified and refiled, with consequent great increase in the survival chances of a man. All its content is contra-survival. When it is gone, survival is demonstrably enhanced—and that means what it says and the fact can be proven in a clinical laboratory with an experiment on the order of "is this water?"

Pleasure memories can be attacked with various techniques. But they are set. They won't budge. Refile the reactive memories and the whole conscious lifetime of the individual springs into view, brilliant and clear, unmodified by the by-pass circuits which are madness. Reduce the reactive bank and the optimum mind for the individual comes into view. The reactive bank was neither the drive nor the personality of the individual—these are indelible and inherent.

And another thing happens. The by-pass circuits and the reactive bank apparently stand only between the conscious banks and the analyzer. They do not stand between, for instance, the ear and the sonic file in the conscious bank, the eye and the visio file, et cetera. This is a very important discovery in its own right, for it means that an aberration, for instance, about the inability to hear did not prevent all proper sound from being filed, about the inability to see color did not prevent all color from being filed. Clear away the reactive circuit which apparently prevented the observations and the analyzer finds itself possessed of whole banks of material it never knew it had, all in proper sound and color, et al.

For instance, a man who supposes that the whole world is ugly and sordid is guided through therapy. The aberration which made the world seem ugly and sordid folds up when the engram or engrams to that effect de-intensify and refile. The by-pass circuit these engrams caused to be set up did *not* prevent a full, true recording to be made, via all sensory channels. Therefore, when the analyzer is permitted to enter the files, the individual discovers that he has innumerable pleasurable experiences which, when they occurred, appeared to him to be ugly and sordid but which are now bright.

This postulates another circumstance, interesting but not vital to Dianetics. The standard memory banks of the mind are evidently not filled with memories which are entities capable of willy-nilly determinism on the individual. They are not automatically restimulated by the perception of something which suggests them in the environment. They are not hooked into circuit on a permanent basis at all. They are filled with conclusions and the analyzer may pick up the old conclusions or create new ones which change the old. In other words, *the standard bank is at the command of the analyzer and the individual; the individual is not at the command of the standard banks.*

In short there is no such thing as conditioning. Conditioning is all right for rats and dogs and cats. They run on the reactive type bank. Therefore what we refer to, ordinarily, as conditioning, is actually an engram command laid down in a specific moment. This is easily susceptible of clinical proof. The conditioning of a lifetime on the subject, say, of eating with a knife, breaks down the instant that the engram command demanding it is de-intensified.

This is not theory, but actuality: conditioning in the absence of engrams on the subject does not and cannot exist. Conditioning can be removed and will stay removed. There are then two things at work: the reactive mind commands certain actions and these can be altered by the de-intensification of engrams. The analyzer can hook up and arrange certain automatic responses for various mechanical situations and actions. Call the reactive mind demand a habit, call the analytical requirement a training pattern. There are habits: these can be removed. There are training patterns: these can be altered only with the consent of the analyzer, which is to say, the individual. Practically all the survival patterns which really lead to survival are laid down on the analytical level. The reactions in which people indulge which are contra-survival are laid down on the reactive level.

Conditioning, therefore, is another term which can be laid aside. The analyzer, working without impedance by engrams, can lay down or take up training patterns at will. The reactive mind can lay down commands which make habits only when the exterior world implants such commands in the absence of full analytical power. Dianetics can break up habits, simply by relieving the engrams which command them. Dianetics could only change a training pattern if the individual consented to it.

These discoveries were an additional proof that Man was a self-determined individual. Further investigation led to another finding; that although the reactive bank was exterior determinism this determinism was a variable on the individual. In other words, the determinism laid in by pain had a variable effect. The same engram introduced into three different people might bring about three different reactions. Man is so thoroughly a self-determined organism that he has a variable reaction to all attempted determinisms. Research brought out the fact that he could exercise a power of choice over the reactive bank, even if in a limited manner. He had five ways to handle an engram: he could attack it and its counterpart in the exterior world, he could flee from it and its counterpart, he could avoid it and its counterpart, he could neglect it and its counterpart, or he could succumb to it. He was self-determined to some degree within this group of reactions. And these are the reactions to any dangerous, contra-survival problem.

These are, by the way, known as the "black panther mechanisms" in Dianetic parlance. Imagine that a black panther is sitting on the stairs. There are five ways of handling the situation for a man sitting in the living room and who has a desire to go upstairs. He could attack the panther, he could flee from it, he could avoid it by going outside and coming up via the porch lattice—or entice the panther away as another method of avoidance—he could simply refuse to admit it was a black panther and attempt to go up anyway, or he could simply lie still in fear paralysis and hope that the black panther would either eat him quietly without too much pain or merely walk off in antipathy to corpses. (Fear-paralysis, denial of dangerousness.)

Now an analyzer does not handle conscious level—standard bank—memories in this fashion. The analyzer evaluates the present and future in terms of experience and education of the past plus imagination. The standard bank is used for computation, not for emotional reaction, guilt, self-revilement, et cetera. The only valid data is that data in the standard bank and in its search for success, happiness, pleasure or whatever desirable end or merely in the art of contemplation, the analyzer must have reliable information and observation. It uses memory, conclusions drawn from experience and conclusions drawn from its conclusions and computes in various ways to obtain correct answers. It avoids a false datum as a curse once it knows it is false. And it is constantly re-evaluating the memory files to reform conclusions. The more experience it has, the better its answers. Bad experience is fine data for computation because it brings in the necessity level. But the analyzer *cannot* compute reactive data, the "unconscious memories" it cannot reach and does not even know about.

So these reactive "memories" aren't memories at all as we understand *memory*. They are something else. They were never meant to be recalled on the analytical level or to be analyzed in any way. The analyzer, trying to get around that red-tab bank sets up some circuits which would tax a Rube Goldberg to duplicate. The analyzer is trying to reach its proper conscious level banks. If it can't, it can't compute right answers. If the analyzer keeps getting strange and seemingly sourceless material which nevertheless has pain to enforce its acceptance, that analyzer can get very wrong answers. And the structural body can go wrong. And motives go wrong. And somebody invents phrases like "it's human to err".

No, reactive "memories" aren't memories. So we call them by a good medical term, *engrams*—a lasting trace—and modify the definition by qualifying "lasting". They were certainly lasting enough, pre-Dianetics.

The engram is received, we can postulate, on a cellular level. The engram is cellular memory by the cells and stored in the cells. We won't go further with this because at present we want to stay out of the problems of structure. But we can prove to anyone's satisfaction that the reactive mind bank is apparently inside the cells themselves, and is not part of the human mind banks which are composited of, we suppose, nerve cells. Engrams are in any kind of cell in the whole aggregation. They do not in the least depend upon nervous structure to exist. They use and prey upon nervous structure as we know it. So we are not talking about memory when we talk about engrams. We are talking about cellular recordings on the order of phonograph records, smell records, organic sensation records, all very precise. And when we say reactive mind we are talking about no special part of the body but a composite, cellular level moronic method of remembering and computing. Someday somebody may cut off a chunk of brain and cry, "Eureka, this is the reactive mind". Possibly. But staying with our functional computation, we can make good time and get workable results. And so we need to know no seat for the reactive mind. And we need to know nothing about the exact structure of its banks. All we want to know is what they do.

The reactive engram comes in with pain when the analytical mind is more or less out of circuit. The engram is *not* recorded in the conscious level banks. It comes in on a cellular level, just as though the cells which compose the body, suddenly recognizing that the organism is in apparent danger of perishing, grab data in an effort to save themselves on the order of a disintegrated, every man for himself, effort. But the data they get is not disordered. It is most terribly precise, most alarmingly literal. It is exact. "Bean" means "bean" in all the ways the sound of "bean" can mean "bean".

Once received, this engram can then lie dormant, inactive. It takes a remotely similar, conscious level experience to stir that engram up. This key-in moment evidently refiles the engram within the red-tab banks and gives it articulation. The words of the engram get meaning. The perceptions get hooked into the sensory organs. The engram is now in place. After this it can be very easily restimulated. The cells are now capable of back-seat driving.

Well, these are the discoveries. Once they had been made it was necessary to find out how they could be applied.

Man, we have postulated—and it is certainly working—is obeying the basic command, SURVIVE!

Dianetics:

This is a dynamic command. It demands action. In looking over the matter of obedience to this command numerous computations were necessary. Survive. Well, the first answer and the too obvious one is that Man is surviving as a unit organism. A very thorough computation on this—about two hundred thousand words—revealed the fact that while everything in the Universe could be explained—by a few shifty turns of logic—in terms of personal survival, the thing was unwieldy and unworkable. We want things to be workable. This is engineering, not idle study. We have a definite goal. So let us see if Man is all out for Man.

The whole reason for the organism's survival *can* be computed down into this single effort, the survival of contemporary Mankind. All the reason a unit organism survives is to let all Mankind survive. But that does not work well.

Now let us take a group, under which we put symbiotes.* Let us postulate that the unit organism survives wholly for the group. Again, a computation can be made that explains everything down to group.

Symbiotes: those organisms which are interdependent for their survival; all entities and energies which aid survival.

Group is the only reason, says this computation. It's unwieldy but there's nothing wrong with it.

All right, let's try bringing it all down to sex. And still it can be computed perfectly, if it is a trifle unwieldy. The reason Man as a unit survives is to enjoy sex and create posterity. But it requires an enormous number of heavy, cumbersome manipulations of logic that no one would like.

Investigating in the mind—going to the object one is studying and really examining it instead of windily arguing about it and quoting authority—it was discovered that an apparent balance existed only when and if *all four drives* were relatively in force. Each one computed well enough, but taken as the four-fold goal they balance. The computing becomes very simple. Behavior begins to look good. Using all four, we can predict.

Now comes the proof. Can we use it? Does it work? It does. Engrams lie across these drives. They have their own energy, these engrams, a reverse polarity surcharge which inhibits the drive on which they lie. This is very schematic but it computes and we can use it in therapy. An unconscious period containing physical pain and conceived or actual antagonism to survival thwarts or blocks or impedes the flow of drive force. Begin to stack up these impedances on a drive and it begins to damp markedly.

Now comes arithmetic. There's a good reason to use the figure four. There are four drives. There are four levels of physical tone. If a man's composite drive force is considered as four and his restimulated—acute or chronic, either way—reactive mind force is high enough to reduce that composite drive force below two, *the individual is insane.* In view of the fact that an engram can be currently restimulated to reduce that force below two, a condition of temporary insanity results.

An engram can consist of father beating mother during a child's anaten. When this engram is highly restimulated, the child, now an adult, may possibly dramatize it either as the father or the mother and will carry out the full drama, *word for word, blow for blow.*

In view of the fact that when father beat mother, father was probably dramatizing one of his own engrams, another factor can be found here which is highly interesting. It is contagion. *Engrams are contagious.* Papa has an engram. He beats mother into anaten. She now has an engram word for word from him. The child was anaten, maybe booted aside and knocked out. The child is part of mother's perceptics for that engram. Mother dramatizes the engram on the child. The child has the engram. He dramatizes it on another child. When adulthood is attained, the engram is dramatized over and over. Contagion.

Why do societies degenerate? A race comes to a new place. New life, few restimulators—a restimulator being the environment's equivalent to the engram's perceptic content—and high necessity level which means high drive. The race thrives on the new frontier. And then begins this contagion, already present, brought in part from the old environment. And the descending spiral can be observed.

Having an engram makes one slightly anaten. Being slightly anaten one more easily receives new engrams. Engrams carry physical pain—psychosomatics—which reduces the general tone and brings on further anaten. And in a rapidly descending spiral, the individual decays.

These were the computations achieved by research and investigation. Now it came to making them work. If they didn't work, we'd have to change things and get new principles. It happens that the above works.

But to start them working was a difficult thing. There was no way of knowing how many engrams a patient might have. One could be cheerfully optimistic by this time. After all, there was a pretty good computation, some knowledge of the nature of the black enchantment, and it might be possible to bring about a "Clear"—optimum working condition of the analyzer—in almost any patient. But the road was full of stones.

Several techniques were developed all of which brought alleviation approximating a couple of thousand hours of psychoanalysis. But that wasn't good enough. They could bring about better results than hypno-analysis and bring them about much more easily. But that wasn't getting the train over the stream.

I found out about locks. A lock is a situation of mental anguish. It depends for its force on the engram to which it is appended. The lock is more or less known to the analyzer. It's a moment of severe restimulation of an engram. Psychoanalysis might be called a study of the locks. I discovered that any patient I had had thousands upon thousands of locks, enough to keep me busy forever. Removal of locks alleviates. It even knocks down chronic psychosomatic ills—at times. It produces more results than anything else so far known elsewhere, but it doesn't *cure*. Removal of locks does not give the individual all his mental powers back, his audio-tone, visio-color, smell, taste, organic memory and imagination. And it doesn't particularly increase his I.Q. I knew that I was far from the optimum analyzer.

It was necessary to go back and back in the lives of patients looking for real engrams, total anaten. Many were found. Some were found that would release when the patient was removed in time back to them and was made to go over and over them, perceptic by perceptic. But there were also engrams that would not release, and they should have, if the original computation was correct. The optimum computer must analyze the data on which it operates, and, once false data have been called to its attention for questioning, the self-checking feature of the computer should automatically reject that falsity.

89

Dianetics:

The fact that an engram wouldn't release worried me: either the basic idea that the brain was a perfect computer was wrong, or—hm-m-m. Before too long it was found that one had to have the first instant of each perceptic before the later engram would go. That looked like order. Get the earliest pain associated with, for instance, a squeaking street car wheel, and later street car wheels, even in bad engrams, gave no trouble. The perfect computer wouldn't overcome the short circuit at level 256 if the same circuit was shorted at level 21, but clear the short circuit— the false data—where it first appeared, and then the computer could readily find and correct the later errors.

Then began the most persistent search possible to find the earliest engram in any patient. This was mad work. Utterly weird.

One day I found myself with a complete birth engram on my hands. At first I did not know what it was. Then there was the doctor's patter. There was the headache, the eyedrops—Hello! People can remember birth when they're properly bucked into it! Aha! Birth's the earliest engram. Everybody has a birth. We'll all be Clears!

Ah, if it had been true! Everybody has a birth. And believe me, birth is quite an experience, very aberrative. Causes asthma and eyestrain and somatics galore. Birth is no picnic and the child is sometimes furious, sometimes apathetic but definitely recording, definitely a human being with a good idea of what's happening when he isn't anaten. And when the engram rises, he knows analytically all about it. (And he can dramatize it, if he's a doctor or she can dramatize it, if she's a mother.) But birth isn't all the answer. Because people didn't become Clears and stop stuttering and stop having ulcers and stop being aberrated and stop having demon circuits when birth was lifted. And sometimes birth didn't lift.

The last was enough for me. There was an axiom: find the earliest engram. Know where it wound up? *Shortly before conception*, for a body. Not all cases, fortunately. Some cases waited four days after conception before they got their first engram. The embryo anatens easily; evidently *there is cellular anaten.*

No statement as drastic as this—as far beyond previous experience as this—can be accepted readily.* I have no explanation of the structure involved; for the engineering answer of function, however, structural explanation is not immediately necessary. I was after one and only one thing: a technical process whereby aberrations could be eliminated, and the full potentiality of the computational ability of the mind restored. If that process involved accepting provisionally that human cells achieve awareness on the order of cellular engrams as little as a day or two after conception, then for the purposes at hand that proposition can, and must, be accepted. If it had been necessary to go back through two thousand years of genetic memory, I would still be going back to find that first engram—but fortunately there's no genetic memory, as such. But there definitely is something which the individual's mind regards as prenatal engrams. Their objective reality can be debated by anyone who chooses to do so; their subjective reality is beyond debate—so much so that the process works when, only when, and *invariably when* we accept the

---

*Validating this work, medical authorities have since released much data on the phenomena discovered by Hubbard concerning both birth and prenatal engrams, and are read about even in such magazines as Time, Reader's Digest, and the Ladies Home Journal. What was so novel then has become well accepted since.

reality of those prenatal memories. We are seeking a process that cures aberrations, not an explanation of the universe, the function of life, or anything else. Therefore we accept as a working—because it works—postulate that *prenatal engrams are recorded as early as shortly before conception.* The objective reality has been checked so far as time and limited means permitted. And the objective reality of prenatal engrams is evidently quite valid. Any psychologist can check this if he knows Dianetic technique and can find some twins separated at birth. But even if he found discrepancies the bald fact remains that individuals *cannot* be rehabilitated unless the prenatal engrams are accepted.

What happens to a child in a womb? The commonest events are accidents, illnesses—and *attempted abortions!*

Call the last an AA. Where do people get ulcers? In the womb usually, AA. Full registry of all perceptics down to the last syllable, material which can be fully dramatized. The largest part of the proof is that lifting the engram of such an event *resolves the ulcer!*

How does the fetus heal up with all this damage? Ask a doctor about twenty years hence—I've got my

93

hands full. That's structure, and right now all I want is a Clear.

What's that chronic cough? That's mama's cough which compressed the baby into anaten when he was five days after conception. She said it hurt and happened all the time. So it did. What's arthritis? Fetal damage or embryo damage.

It so happens, it is now known, that a Clear can control all his body fluids. In an aberree the reactive mind does a job of that. The reactive mind says things have to be such and so and that's survival. So a man grows a withered arm. That's survival. Or he has inability to see, hysterical or actual blindness. That's survival. Sure it is. Good solid sense. Had an engram about it, didn't he?

What's TB? Predisposition of the respiratory system to infection. What's this, what's that? You've got the proposition now. It works. The psycho-somatic ills, the arthritis, the impotence, this and that, they go away when the engrams are cleared from the bottom.

That was the essence of the derivation of the technical process. With the research stage completed the actual application was the remaining stage, and the gathering of data on the final, all-important question. The process worked—definitely and unequivocally worked. But the full definition of a science requires that it permit accurate description of how to produce a desired result *invariably*. Would the technique work on all types of minds, on every case?

By early 1950 over two hundred patients had been tested; of those two hundred people, two hundred cures had been obtained. Dianetics is a science because by following readily prescribed techniques, which can be specifically stated, based on definitely stated basic postulates, a specifically described result can be obtained in every case. There may, conceivably, be exceptions to the technique now worked out, but I tried honestly to find exceptions and did not; that's why I tried so many cases, of so many different types. And some of them were really gruesome cases.

Who is an aberree? Anybody who has one or more engrams. And since birth itself is a very engramic experience—every human being born has at least one engram!

Dianetics:

The whole world, according to the hypnotist, needs nothing but to be hypnotized. Just put another engram, an artificial one, into a man, even if it's a manic engram—makes the subject "big" or "strong" or "powerful" plus all other perceptics contained—and he's all right. That's the basic trouble. Reduction of self-determinism. So we don't use hypnotism. Besides, it's not workable on any high percentage. If you've followed this far without realizing that we are trying to wake up an analyzer, you made the same mistake I did for many months. I tried to work with hypnosis. Well, it works, after a sloppy fashion. But how you put a man to sleep who is already three-quarters asleep—normal, near as I can discover—is a problem I wish could be solved. But fortunately it doesn't need solution.

The analyzer went to sleep with each engram. Each engram had lock engrams—like it, also engrams, but subsequent to it—and each chain of engrams (same species—people have about fifteen or twenty chains on the average, of ten or fifteen engrams to the chain) has about a thousand locks. There are luckless people who have hundreds of engrams. They may be sane. There are people who have twenty engrams and are insane. There are people who are sane for years and suddenly get into just the right environment and get restimulated and go mad. And anybody who has an engram he has had fully restimulated has been mad—vox populi—for at least once, even if only for ten minutes.

When we start to treat a person, we are treating a partially asleep analyzer—and the problem is to wake him up in the first engram and then erase—that's right *erase*, they vanish out of the reactive bank on recounting over and over with each perceptic—all subsequent engrams. The locks blow out without being touched, the Doctrine of the True Datum working full blast and the analyzer refusing to tolerate what it suddenly notices to be nonsense. And as he recovers mental function enough to reach back a little way into his past, we begin to alleviate. Then we finally find out the reactive mind plot—why he had to keep on being aberrated—and we blow out the demons—upsetting the circuits—and all of a sudden we are at basic basic, first engram. Then we come forward, recounting each engram over and over until it blows away and refiles as experience as opposed to command.

A Clear has regression recall. Basic personality, in an aberree, isn't strong enough to go back so we use

97

Dianetics:

what we call the *Dianetic reverie*.*

We found why narco-synthesis is so sloppy. It puts the partially restimulated engram into full restimulation, keys all of it in. The drug turns off the somatic—physical pain—so that it doesn't wholly go away. And narco has no chance of going back far enough to get basic basic and the one it reaches will pretend to erase and then will surge back in from sixty hours to sixty days.

Does any special thing hold up a case? Yes, the sympathy computation. Patient had a tough engramic background, then broke his leg and got sympathy. Thereafter he tends to go around with a simulated broken leg—arthritis, et cetera, et cetera. These are hard to crack sometimes, but they should be cracked first. They make a patient "want to be sick". Sickness has a high survival value says the reactive mind. So it tailors up a body to be sick, good and sick. Allies are usually grandmothers who protested against the child being aborted—effort already made, child listening in, not knowing the words just then but he'll know them later when he

Reverie: a light state of concentration not to be confused with hypnosis. In reverie the person is fully aware of what is taking place.

knows his first words—nurses who were very kind; doctors who bawled mama out, et cetera, et cetera. Patient usually has an enormous despair charge around the loss of an ally. That'll hold up a case.

We've completely by-passed how this ties in with modern psychology. After all, modern psychology has labels for many observed conditions. How about schizophrenia, for instance?

That's valence.* An aberree has a valence for every person in every engram. He has basically three, himself, mother and father. Every engram has dramatic personnel. A valence builds up in the reactive mind and walls off a compartment, absorbing some of the analyzer—which is shut down by restimulation. Multi-valence is common to every aberree. The valence of every aberree gets shifted day to day depending upon whom he meets. He tries to occupy the top dog valence in every engramic dramatization. Taking this is the highest survival computation that can be made by the reactive mind; always win. Break a dramatization and you break the patient into another valence. If you break him down

Valence: the characteristics of one individual unwittingly assumed by another.

to being himself in that engram he will probably go anaten or get sick. Keep breaking his dramatizations and he is disabled mentally.

Who will practice Dianetics? In severe cases, doctors. They are well schooled in the art of healing, they are always being bombarded by psycho-somatics and mental situations. The doctor has, like the engineer, a certain necessity for results. There are several methods of alleviation which will work in a few hours, break up a chronic illness in a child, change valences, change a person's position on the time track—people get caught in various places where the command says to be caught—alter drama-tization pattern and generally handle the sick aberree.

In the general case, however—the psychosomatic, neurotic, or merely sub-optimum individual—Dian-etics will probably be practiced by people of intel-ligence and good drive on their friends and families. Knowing all the axioms and mechanisms, Dianetics is easy to apply to the fairly normal individual and can relieve his occlusions and colds and arthritis and other psychosomatic ills. It can be used as well to prevent aberrations from occurring and can even be applied to determine the reactions of others.

Although the fundamentals and mechanisms are simple and, with some study, very easily applied, partial information is dangerous, the technique may be the stuff of which sanity is made but one is after all engaging action with the very stuff which creates madness and he should at least inform himself with a few hours study before he experiments.

I have discussed here the evolution of Dianetics. Actually I have concentrated upon Abnormal Dianetics. There are Medical Dianetics, Dynamic Dianetics—drives and structure—Political Dianetics, Military Dianetics, Industrial Dianetics, et cetera, et cetera, and not the least PREVENTIVE DIANETICS. On that may hang the final answer to society.

And now as an epilogue, Dianetics is summarized in its current workable form. It does the following things, based on an ample series of cases:

1. Dianetics is an organized science of thought built on definite axioms; it apparently reveals the existence of natural laws by which behavior can uniformly be caused or predicted in the unit organism or society.

2. Dianetics offers a therapeutic technique with

which we can treat any and all inorganic mental and organic psychosomatic ills, with assurance of complete cure in unselected cases. It produces a mental stability in the "cleared" patient which is far superior to the current norm. (This statement is accurate to date; it is conceded that further work may demonstrate some particular case somewhere which may not entirely respond.)

3. In Dianetics we have a method of time dislocation dissimilar to narco-synthesis or hypnosis which is called the Dianetic reverie; with it the patient is able to reach events hitherto hidden from him, erasing the physical and mental pain from his life.

4. Dianetics gives us an insight into the potential capabilities of the mind.

5. Dianetics reveals the basic nature of Man and his purposes and intents, with the discovery that these are basically constructive and not evil.

6. Dianetics gives us an appreciation of the magnitude of events necessary to aberrate an individual.

7. With Dianetics we discover the nature of

pre-natal experience and its precise effect upon the post-natal individual.

8. Dianetics discovered the actual aberration factors of birth.

9. Dianetics elucidates the entire problem of "unconsciousness" and demonstrates conclusively that "total unconsciousness" does not exist short of death.

10. Dianetics shows that all memories of all kinds are recorded fully and retained.

11. Dianetics demonstrates that aberrative memories lie only in areas of "unconsciousness" and, conversely, that only "unconscious" memories are capable of aberrating.

12. Dianetics opens broad avenues for research and poses numerous problems for solution. One new field, for instance, is the sub-science of Perceptics—the structure and function of perceiving and identifying stimuli.

13. Dianetics sets forth the non-germ theory of disease, embracing, it has been estimated by com-

petent physicians, the cure of some seventy percent of Man's pathology.

14. Dianetics offers hope that the destruction of the function of the brain, by shock or surgery, will no longer be a necessary evil.

15. Dianetics offers a workable explanation of the various physiological effects of drugs and endocrine substances and points out numerous answers to former endocrine problems.

16. Dianetics gives a more fundamental explanation of the uses, principles and fundamentals of hypnotism and similar mental phenomena.

17. To sum up, Dianetics proposes and experimentally supports a new viewpoint on Man and his behavior. It carries with it the necessity of a new sort of mental hygiene. It indicates a new method of approach to the solution of the problems which confront governments, social agencies, industries, and, in short, Man's sphere of endeavor. It suggests new fields of research. Finally it offers a glimmer of hope that Man may continue his process of evolution toward a higher organism without straying toward the danger point of his own destruction.

This is part of the story of the search. I have given the story as it is and the major results exactly as they turned out.

Man's efforts to free man by enslaving him in social and personal aberrations was the wrong equation. The road to nowhere. In the ages past—building up since before Egypt's time—the hold of this slavery of aberration has been broken momentarily only, by the opening up of new lands and the appearance of new races.

But now we've got a science to break it and a technology to be applied.

Up there are the stars. Down in the arsenal is an atom bomb.

Which one is it going to be?

Note

A much more detailed account of this search and the processes which resolve it are contained in *Dianetics: The Modern Science of Mental Health* by L. Ron Hubbard. (See book list, page 111.)

The Fundamental Axioms of Dianetics*

The dynamic principle of existence—SURVIVE!

Survival, considered as the single and sole Purpose, subdivides into four dynamics.

DYNAMIC ONE is the urge of the individual toward survival for the individual and his symbiotes. (By symbiote is meant all entities and energies which aid survival.)

DYNAMIC TWO is the urge of the individual toward survival through procreation; it includes both the sex act and the raising of progeny, the care of children and their symbiotes.

DYNAMIC THREE is the urge of the individual toward survival for the group or the group for the group and includes the symbiotes of that group.

DYNAMIC FOUR is the urge of the individual toward survival for Mankind or the urge toward survival of Mankind for Mankind as well as the group for Mankind, etc., and includes the symbiotes of Mankind.

The absolute goal of survival is immortality or infinite survival. This is sought by the individual in terms of himself as an organism, as a spirit or as a name or as his children, as a group of which he is a member or as Mankind and the progeny and symbiotes of others as well as his own.

The reward of survival activity is pleasure.

*From *Dianetics: The Modern Science of Mental Health* by L. Ron Hubbard.

The ultimate penalty of destructive activity is death or complete nonsurvival, and is pain.

Successes raise the survival potential toward infinite survival. Failures lower the survival potential toward death.

The human mind is engaged upon perceiving and retaining data, composing or computing conclusions and posing and resolving problems related to organisms along all four dynamics and the purpose of perception, retention, concluding and resolving problems is to direct its own organism and symbiotes and other organisms and symbiotes along the four dynamics toward survival.

Intelligence is the ability to perceive, pose and resolve problems.

The dynamic is the tenacity to life and vigor and persistence in survival.

Both the dynamic and intelligence are necessary to persist and accomplish and neither is a constant quantity from individual to individual, group to group.

The dynamics are inhibited by engrams, which lie across them and disperse life force.

Intelligence is inhibited by engrams which feed false or improperly graded data into the analyzer.

Happiness is the overcoming of not unknown obstacles toward a known goal and, transiently, the contemplation of or indulgence in pleasure.

The analytical mind is that portion of the mind which perceives and retains experience data to compose and resolve problems and direct the organism along the four dynamics.

108

It thinks in differences and similarities.

The reactive mind is that portion of the mind which files and retains physical pain and painful emotion and seeks to direct the organism solely on a stimulus-response basis. It thinks only in identities.

The somatic mind is that mind which, directed by the analytical or reactive mind, places solutions into effect on the physical level.

A training pattern is that stimulus-response mechanism resolved by the analytical mind to care for routine activity or emergency activity. It is held in the somatic mind and can be changed at will by the analytical mind.

Habit is that stimulus-response reaction dictated by the reactive mind from the content of engrams and put into effect by the somatic mind. It can be changed only by those things which change engrams.

Aberrations, under which is included all deranged or irrational behavior, are caused by engrams. They are stimulus-response pro- and contra-survival.

Psychosomatic ills are caused by engrams.

The engram is the single source of aberrations and psychosomatic ills.

Moments of "unconsciousness" when the analytical mind is attenuated in greater or lesser degree are the only moments when engrams can be received.

The engram is a moment of "unconsciousness" containing physical pain or painful emotion and all perceptions and is not available to the analytical mind as experience.

Emotion is three things: engramic response to situations, endocrine metering of the body to meet situations on an analytical level and the inhibition or the furtherance of life force. The potential value of an individual or a group may be expressed by the equation

$$PV = ID^x$$

where I is Intelligence and D is Dynamic.

The worth of an individual is computed in terms of the alignment, on any dynamic, of his potential value with optimum survival along that dynamic. A high PV may, by reversed vector, result in a negative worth as in some severely aberrated persons. A high PV on any dynamic assures a high worth only in the unaberrated person.

CONTACT YOUR NEAREST
SCIENTOLOGY ORGANIZATION

UNITED STATES

ADVANCED ORGANIZATION

Church of Scientology
Advanced Organization
of Los Angeles (AOLA)
1306 N. Berendo Street
Los Angeles, California 90027

SAINT HILL ORGANIZATION

Church of Scientology
American Saint Hill
Organization (ASHO)
1413 N. Berendo Street
Los Angeles, California 90027

PUBLICATIONS ORGANIZATION

Church of Scientology
Publications Organization U.S.
4833 Fountain avenue,
East Annex
Los Angeles, California 90029

LOCAL CHURCHES

AUSTIN
Church of Scientology
2804 Rio Grande
Austin, Texas 78705

BOSTON
Church of Scientology
448 Beacon Street
Boston, Massachusetts 02215

BUFFALO
Church of Scientology
1116 Elmwood Avenue
Buffalo, New York 14222

CHICAGO
Church of Scientology
839 Chicago Avenue
Evanston, Illinois 60202

DENVER
Church of Scientology
375 S. Navajo
Denver, Colorado 80223

DETROIT
Church of Scientology
3905 Rochester Road
Royal Oak, Michigan 48067

HONOLULU
Church of Scientology
143 Nenue Street
Honolulu, Hawaii 96821

LAS VEGAS
Church of Scientology
846 E. Sahara
Las Vegas, Nevada 89104

LOS ANGELES
Church of Scientology
4810 Sunset Boulevard
Los Angeles, California 90027

Church of Scientology
Celebrity Centre Los Angeles
1551 N. La Brea
Hollywood, California 90028

MIAMI
Church of Scientology
120 Giralda
Coral Gables, Florida 33134

NEW YORK
Church of Scientology
28–30 West 74th Street
New York, New York 10023

PHILADELPHIA
Church of Scientology
8 West Lancaster Avenue
Ardmore, Pennsylvania 19003

PHOENIX
Church of Scientology
908 E. Camelback Road
Phoenix, Arizona 85014

PORTLAND
Church of Scientology
333 South West Park Avenue
Portland, Oregon 97205

SACRAMENTO
Church of Scientology
825 15th Street
Sacramento, California 95814

SAN DIEGO
Church of Scientology
348 Olive Street
San Diego, California 92103

SAN FRANCISCO
Church of Scientology
83 MacAllister
San Francisco, California 94102

SEATTLE
Church of Scientology
1318 2nd Avenue
Seattle, Washington 98101

ST. LOUIS
Church of Scientology
3730 Lindell Boulevard
St. Louis, Missouri 63108

TWIN CITIES
Church of Scientology
2708 E. Lake Street
Minneapolis, Minnesota 55406

WASHINGTON, D.C.
Founding Church
of Scientology
2125 "S" Street, N.W.
Washington, D.C. 20008

CANADA

LOCAL CHURCHES

MONTREAL
Church of Scientology
15 Notre Dame Ouest
Montreal, Quebec H2Y 1B5

OTTAWA
Church of Scientology
124 O'Connor St., 4th Floor
Ottawa, Ontario K1P 5M9

TORONTO
Church of Scientology
385 Yonge Street
Toronto, Ontario M5R 2H5

VANCOUVER
Church of Scientology
1130 Granville Street
Vancouver 10,
British Columbia V6V 1M1

MEXICO

Instituto de Filosofia Aplicada
Havre N°. 32, Col. Juarez
Mexico 6, D.F. Mexico

UNITED KINGDOM

ADVANCED ORGANIZATION/
SAINT HILL

Hubbard College
of Scientology
Advanced Organization
Saint Hill (AOSH UK)
Saint Hill Manor
East Grinstead, Sussex
RH19 4JY
England

LOCAL CHURCHES

EAST GRINSTEAD
Saint Hill Foundation
Saint Hill Manor
   East Grinstead, Sussex,
   RH19 4JY
England

LONDON
Hubbard Scientology
   Organization
68 Tottenham Court Road
London W.1, England

MANCHESTER
Hubbard Scientology
   Organization
48 Faulkner Street
Manchester M1 4FH, England

PLYMOUTH
Hubbard Scientology
   Organization
39 Portland Square
Sherwell, Plymouth
Devon, England PL4 6DJ

EDINBURGH
Hubbard Academy
   of Personal Independence
Fleet House
20 South Bridge
Edinburgh, Scotland EH1 1LL

EUROPE

ADVANCED ORGANIZATION

Church of Scientology
Advanced Organization
   Europe
Jernbanegade 6
1608 Copenhagen V, Denmark

SAINT HILL ORGANIZATION

Church of Scientology
Saint Hill Europe
Jernbanegade 6
1608 Copenhagen V, Denmark

PUBLICATIONS ORGANIZATION

Scientology Publications
   Organization Denmark
Store Kongensgade 55,
1264 Copenhagen K, Denmark

LOCAL CHURCHES

AMSTERDAM
Church of Scientology
Nieuwe Zijds Voorburgwal 312
1012RV Amsterdam, Holland

AUSTRIA
Scientology Österreich
Mariahilferstrasse 88a
11 Unterteil,
A-1010 Vienna, Austria

BERN
Church of Scientology
2 Sudbahnhofstrasser
3007 Bern, Switzerland

COPENHAGEN
Scientology Kirken, Danmark
Vesterbrogade 23A-25
1620 Copenhagen V, Denmark

Scientology Kirken,
   Copenhagen
Frederiksborgvej 5
2400 Copenhagen NV,
   Denmark

GÖTEBORG
Church of Scientology
Küngsgatan 23,
S-411 19 Göteborg, Sweden

MALMÖ
Church of Scientology
Stortorget 27-29,
S-211 34 Malmö, Sweden

MILANO
Hubbard Dianetics Institute
Galleria del Corso 4
20100 Milano, Italy

MUNICH
Church of Scientology
8000 Munchen 2
Lindwurmstrasse 29
Munich, West Germany

PARIS
Church of Scientology
12 Rue de la Montagne
Ste. Genevieve 75005
Paris, France

STOCKHOLM
Church of Scientology
Kammakaregatan 46
S-111 60 Stockholm, Sweden

SOUTH AFRICA

LOCAL CHURCHES

BULAWAYO
Church of Scientology
210-211 Kirrie Bldgs.
Cnr. Abercorn & 9th Avenue
Bulawayo, Rhodesia

CAPETOWN
Church of Scientology
3rd Floor Garmour House
127 Plein Street
Capetown, South Africa 8001

DURBAN
Church of Scientology
57 College Lane
Durban, South Africa 4001

JOHANNESBURG
Church of Scientology
99 Polly Street
Johannesburg, South Africa
   2001

PORT ELIZABETH
Church of Scientology
2 St. Christopher's
27 West Bourne Road
Port Elizabeth, South Africa
   6001

PRETORIA
Church of Scientology
224 Central House
Cnr. Central & Pretora Streets
Pretoris, South Africa 0002

AUSTRALIA/
NEW ZEALAND

LOCAL CHURCHES

ADELAIDE
Church of Scientology
28 Weymouth Street
Adelaide, SA 5000, Australia

MELBOURNE
Church of the New Faith
724 Inkerman Road
North Caulfield 3161
Melbourne, Victoria, Australia

PERTH
Church of Scientology
Pastoral House
156 St. George's Terrace
Perth 6000, Western Australia

SYDNEY
Church of Scientology
1 Lee Street
Sydney 2000
New South Wales, Australia

AUCKLAND
Church of Scientology
New Imperial Buildings
44 Queen Street
Auckland 1, New Zealand